FIRESTORM
A Personal Narrative

Vignettes from the epicenter
of the 2017 Sonoma County Tubbs Firestorm –
one of the most destructive wildfires
in California history

Jon Humboldt Gates

Moonstone Publishing
Copyright 2018

First Printing 2018

Copyright © 2018 Jon Humboldt Gates
All rights reserved

Cover and book design by Renee Davis
Cover and inside photography by Jon Humboldt Gates

ISBN: 978-1-878136-02-2

Printed in the United States
Sheridan Press, Michigan

Moonstone Publishing
P.O. Box 1414, Windsor, CA 95492
jon.humboldt.gates@gmail.com

Remembrance ...

Michel Azarian
Karen Aycock
Carmen Berriz
Irma Bowman
Roy Bowman
George Chaney
Carol Collins-Swasey
Janet Costanzo
Stanley Coolidge, Jr.
David Culp
Michael Dornbach
Valerie Evans
Elizabeth Foster
Jane Gardiner
Mike Grabow
Arthur Grant
Suiko Grant
Donna Halbur
LeRoy Halbur
Roseann Hannah
Christina Hanson
Tak-Fu Hung

Monte Kirven
Sally Lewis
Veronica McCombs
Carmen McReynolds
Garrett Paiz
Sandra Picciano
Lynne Powell
Marilyn Ress
Charles Rippey
Sara Rippey
Sharon Rae Robinson
Lee Rogers
Teresa Santos
Majorie 'Marnie' Schwartz
Kai Shepherd
Kressa Jean Shepherd
Daniel Southard
Steve Stelter
Margaret Stephenson
Edward Stone
Tamara Latrice Thomas
Linda Tunis

Contents

Remembrance …   5

Forward
Prologue (2015)   13
Drought   15
Vestiges   20

Silence Before the Storm
Silence, Before the Storm   25
Inferno   31
Running in the Night   36
Exodus   43
Severed   48
Crow's Nest (Dream)   53
Fields of Gray   56
She   60
Chariste   62
The Ocean   66
Gone   69
Valeen (Dreams)   73
Fire Zombies I   75
Fatal Night   79
M5 Reckoning   81
Torn by the Wind (Dreams)   83
Fire Zombies II   85
And the Angels Came Knocking   87
Aftermath   93

Second Fire
Second Fire   115
Night Hours   117
Demons Between Us   119
Opt Out   121
Failure   125
Battle of Vinograd   128
Sister Cities   130
Sue the Winds   132

Spreadsheets   134
Hail Mary   138
Zombies in the Kitchen   140
Up In the Air   142
Beyond All Logic   147
Redemption   152
The Cloud   155
Jasper in a Clock (Dreams)   157
Corner Stones   158
The Stars   161

Regeneration

Regeneration   166
Landscapes   168
Apollo's Fire   171

Wanderings

Zombies By The Bay   176
Wanderings   180
Settlement Day   182

Acknowledgments   187

Index of Photographs   190

Forward

California was in the grip of a five-year drought when we bought our home in the foothills of the Mayacamas Mountains north of Santa Rosa in 2014. My family had been in Northern California since 1849 and saw droughts come and go over the decades. We were a little skeptical to buy hill country land in the face of a drought, but historic experience showed that patterns break, the rains come back in enormous patterns and the land recovers. California has always been a place of extreme swings, in weather, economy and politics.

The year after we bought our home a series of devastating wild fires broke out across Lake County to the northeast. I sat on the high Sonoma ridges and watched the firestorm thunderheads form over the Valley Fire as it swept across Lake County, driving thousands from their homes. The cycles of change were getting more extreme. It was sobering and chilling, but at a distance it gave me some false sense of security farther west in Sonoma County.

We thought the drought was broken during the winter of 2016, when huge atmospheric rivers rolled in from the Southern Pacific Ocean and unleashed unprecedented volumes of rainfall. Lakes and reservoirs reached maximum capacity. Rainfall records for the region were shattered, reconfirming the notion that California has big swings. The seasonal creeks on our land were running full force with white water rapids and waterfalls. We thought it had broken the back of the drought with a sense of great relief.

But the summer of 2017 returned with a vengeance. It was hot. Very hot. Temperatures on our property reached 115 degrees in September. But we still felt that the seasonal patterns had changed and hoped that one more winter would set the record straight. I will forever remember the evening of October 8, and the winds that came in the night. I'd just returned from a weeklong trip to the East, glad to be home. I was raking up oak leaves outside the front gate of our property that warm Sunday afternoon. The air was very still.

A couple drove up in an SUV to the neighbor's gate. The neighbor's home was for sale. A man and woman got out of the car and walked around with a small dog. They came over to talk with me and ask about the area. They were from the East Bay, looking for a home in Sonoma County. I said it was really a very quiet place and with great neighbors along the road. People look out for each other here, I said. And that the location was ideal, so close to Santa Rosa, the vineyards, the ocean and San Francisco, but not too far in the hills. We chatted in that warm October evening with no idea that it was all about to explode in a few hours.

Prologue (2015)

Drought

Constant

Pressure

Of absence

Absence of water

Of clouds, of change

The skies endlessly clear

Days, precipitously hot

Barometric pressure dead

Every day, every minute

Eroding your sense of balance

Something is terribly wrong

Like that night

The entire sky to the east

Reflecting a crimson glow

In the darkness

Of some hell unleashed

Beyond Geyser's Ridge

20,000 fleeing its wrath

The avalanche of cinders

Cascading down the hillside

Carried by relentless winds

Fueling fire and smoke

Tens of thousands of trees

Gone

Animals in exodus

Demons unleashed

Dreams and labors vanished

Lives lost

Disintegrated into dust and ash

Thermal clouds consumed
In a rage of fury and chaos
That was the Valley Fire
The Rocky Fire
The Jerusalem Fire
That was Lake County
In 2015
Under the tyranny of drought
It haunts conscious thoughts
You lie awake some nights
Listening to life decay
You irrigate in the face of it
Trees and plants wilting
Millions facing extinction
Every conscious moment
The absence of lifeblood
A stark reminder
In a faucet left on
Taking a shower
Brushing your teeth

Recounting the many trips
Outside the drought zone
East
Where the rains pour down
The fields are green
Thunderheads in Texas
Deluges in Manhattan
Cloud bursts across Iowa
Joyous places of refuge
From the drought

Water dropping from the sky
A natural cadence
And you remember
Those Northwestern storms
Along Puget Sound
Rain, taken for granted
Months and months of moisture
The winds blew
Until you could bear no more
Fly to the deserts
To the islands
Southern latitudes
Seek renewal
In sun and heat
But now you harbor
Deepest wishes
For rains restored

The mist, the fogs
Because all has given way
To relentless days of sun
Lizards play, crickets sing
Frogs have retreated
Animals flee high country
Seeking tributaries of water
In populated lands below
They appear in the night
In increasing numbers
Then in the day
As desperation sets in
Survival prevails

Water, evaporating

A drop at a time

Every day, every night

Every hour, every moment

Lifeblood slipping away

Parched in the winds

You are more wary

Something, silently, encroaching

Santa Anas thunder from the east

A tinderbox, awaiting a spark

And there is nothing you can do

Because it is enormous

Relentless, impartial

No reason in its realm

Extracting life

From dry landscape

From soil and all living things

That will perish in its wake

The rich, the poor

The strong, the weak

The defenders

The civilized

The wild

Fleeing in its midst

When something is created

Something else comes

To destroy it all

The fires, vengeful with terror

The drought prolonged

A torturous, slow demise

Insidiously

Creeping into our lives
Our consciousness
Our being
Under threat of extinction
Constricting us slowly
Tightening its grip
On our life, our world
Our ways

Vestiges

Remembering,
The last drought on this land
Over 40 years ago
I was footloose, carefree
Back then
Living an eternal life
All the futurists saying
It would take more
Than a decade to recover
But the rains
Stormed back
To restore lakes and rivers
Subterranean water plains
But this time it feels different
Deeper, more prolonged
Hinting
At some epochal time
Better measured
Generations from now
Global warming
Shadowing the land
Eerie in its silence
As it strangles life
In the forests
The rivers, the fields
Erasing the efforts
Of all those
Who persevered
In times before
A rich and bountiful land
A place where my ancestors

Farmed, fished and mined
In Northern California
For 150 years
This life that held such promise
For so many before my time
But every day
It creeps in
With its haunting song of silence
Growing quieter all around
No wind
No rain
No change
Just dryness, spreading
I lie awake at night
Counting the crickets' cadence
As they orchestrate the demise
Of a once fruitful land
I long for the return
Of the tree frogs
And their celebration
Echoing in the valley
Vestiges of jubilation
To water in our creeks
The return of the rains
And I wonder, how long
I will have to wait?
The specter haunts me
In the night
Follows me in the day
While the only hope
Rests in the clouds
That never come

Silence Before the Storm

Silence, Before the Storm

It was massive

And already on its way

But we didn't know yet

We were in the death zone

The initial frontline of impact

Sunday night

I was lying awake reading

'Alone On the Wall'

Bivouacked, in the world

Of a solo free climber of vertical rock

Who defied imagination

That's when the scent of smoke

Wafted through the open window

I noticed, but kept reading

It was a breezy, balmy

Inland California valley evening

With no clouds and a star-studded sky

We felt safe, in the twilight

Our house, anchored into bedrock

More than a quarter century standing watch

Over the Russian River Valley below

Foothills, of the Mayacamas Mountains

Earlier that evening, my wife and I

Watched the sunset turn tangerine

Against a cobalt blue sky

But twilight fell eerie

As the last rays slipped away

All of the sounds stopped

The earth paused

Like a pressure drop

The silence

No wind

No crickets

No birds

No cars

No dog barks

No coyote howls

No frogs

No voices

No train whistles

No chainsaws

No fox cries

No hawks

It was dead silent

Even the ambient sounds

Of Highway 101

And Mark West Road

Gone

We'd never heard it so quiet before

'Might be earthquake weather?'

We joked nervously, letting it go at that

And listened to the absolute silence

Then

Our neighbor opened and shut a door

You could hear the door knob turn

A latch release

And then the squeak

Of the door's dry hinges

Slowly opening

From a hundred yards away
Through the trees
Then we heard a plane
High overhead in the distance
The wind began to stir
Crickets started up
Sounds were coming back
And with the sounds
Winds started to build
As we sat under the emerging stars
Unaware that something
Was beginning to go wrong
But there would only be silence
During those unsuspecting hours
As the storm gathered in waves
Rolling into the forests, fanning out
Across the brown tinder grasslands
Stealing across dry creek beds
Illuminating the night, its roar building
Gathering its energy
In the hill country to the east
While thousands slept
To the West
Unaware

As I lay reading at 11:30pm
The smoke intensity increased
Now it had my attention
I put the book down
It would never be picked up again
Wind gusts were getting stronger

Starting to rattle deck furniture
And sway oak and redwood trees
I got up and went to the veranda
Looked down to the valley
It was warm
Lights twinkled below
Out west along River Road
Otherwise, it was pitch black
As far as I could see
But the smoke was there
And it was thickening
This smoke seemed different
Not the smoke of the Valley Fire
That drifted down from Lake County
Two years before
A light odor, high overhead
Nor the smoke of the Helena Fire
That came south from the Trinity Alps
Diluted in the winds by miles of travel
This smoke was dense and fresh
Primal, a deeper body to its scent
Alarming in complexity
An ode to wine country
My wife and I went outside
Walked the property with flashlights
Nothing
The dogs were alert, but stayed close
I walked down to the road and looked
I could see three neighboring homes
Again ... Nothing
But the veil of smoke

Creeping everywhere

So I called 911
First time in my life
Dispatcher said they were getting
Hundreds of calls
About smoke and fire
From all over the region
Clear the line, she said
Watch the hills
Look for orange glows
You are on your own
I saw no signs of fire
In the valley below
But I felt the beat
Of a warning drum
A growing sense of alarm
Rushed to the car, drove fast
Down the winding foothill road
To Reibli Valley, over to Mark West
Gunned it up the Mayacamas
East toward Calistoga
On Porter Creek Road
Into higher country
Just above our home
Hitting 70 in a 45 zone
I saw people wandering
Out of their homes
Looking up into the dark sky
Bewildered, not comprehending
What was coming in the night

I had my car roof cracked open
Smoke was getting stronger
I drove fast in the narrow turns
Passed Mark West Lodge
Franz Valley, Safari West
Toward the Petrified Forest
Hit a turn hard
Sudden chill
Disbelief
At the wheel
The scale of it all
Before me

Inferno

Some crimson hell
As far as I could see to the north
Plumes of fire billowed and rose
Smoke spiraled into the night
Blotting out stars
Making a blood moon above
Flames 80, 100 feet tall
I stopped the car
Stepped outside
Felt the hit
From Diablo Winds
Enormous gusts
Carrying destruction
In their midst
Fire balls lifting off
From tree tops
An otherworldly roar
In the distance
A forest disappearing
Consumed in the jaws
Of an inferno
Thundering its way forward
The mountainside ablaze
Insane to contemplate display
Dwarfed me, left me dazed
Cars and people beginning to flee
From Schlictman Road, Porter Creek
Tiny headlights, illuminating
A pathway, a flight to safety

Against a wall of fire

I froze, overwhelmed

Trying to contemplate

Winds of hysteria

Driving flames

Should have been

Banshee screams

Enormous, wild nature

Coming in a rage

Laying waste and reclaim

My chest sinks

A certain realization

That nothing

Would stop this fire's march west

Now, I raced

To get back to our place

Only a mile or so

As the crow flies

But 10 miles on canyon roads

Tires howling into the curves

My mind fogged

Thinking

This can't be happening

Denial setting in

I felt puny

Insignificant in the face

Of the beast

My mind ripping

Every blade of destiny

Leaving me bewildered

Under the stars

Looming uncertainty

Glanced in the mirror

Coming up from behind

A CDF fire truck closing in

At a crazy frenzy pace

Flashing lights to clear the path

I pulled over and let them pass

Then five sheriff's trucks

In the eastbound lane

Lights blazing, but no sirens

Only silence in their wake

Why weren't their sirens blaring!

Got home at midnight

Said we may have to leave our place

Thought we had an hour, maybe two

Couldn't have been more wrong

My phone lit up, with a text

At 12:15am

From RJ

In the neighboring vineyard

"We all have to run now!"

Fire was over the ridge above

Where he and Crystal stood

With their farm manager

Who had a wife and three kids

They were piling the dogs and kids in the cars

Told their guests

To run for their lives

There's no time to waste

It was coming

Shell shocked

I couldn't comprehend
How fire had moved so fast
We wrenched open car doors
Both dogs were scared
We put them in the cars first
Started grabbing a few heirlooms
Paintings, photos, a guitar
Hard discs, computers, an old clock
Fifteen minutes … to preserve a life time
Got a text from our neighbors
Donna and Rod
Over in their new home
In Fountain Grove
Said come stay with us
We hear fires are at your door
Five minutes later they text back
Said, now we're evacuating too
We called our other neighbors
Everybody, on the run
Horns were blaring
As RJ and his people
Descended from the vineyard above
Texting > You've got to make your run!
The smoke was all around
We took one last look at the home
I even locked the front door
A last grasp at hope
In the final seconds
Then we launched
Down the road
Steel gate rolled open

We passed through
And it closed
Like a door slamming
No going back from here
Met another sheriff's truck
Racing up Crystal Drive
Lights flashing
No siren
Surreal silence
It was the beginning
Of another time
And to think
I locked the door

Running in the Night

We were all running in the night
Scattered five counties wide
Under a million stars in the sky
Maelstrom winds
Whipped smoke and uncertainty about
Calls to 911 only cast deepening doubts
As thousands slowly realized
A storm was coming into their lives
There would be no Emergency Alert
A conscious decision made
That put all of us in Death's path
To stumble blindly, toward fate

Some of us ran
Early and purposefully
Alerted by digital warnings
Few of us subscribed to
We had trailers to load animals
Trucks to place our larger things
Our bags were packed for hours
We rallied ahead of the storm
Helped others when we could
Before the evacuations ensued
We networked with neighbors
Relatives, friends and strangers
We were prepared to run
But we were only a few

We were all running in the night

Some of us ran before smoke and ash
We were in the hill country
Fires leapt Mark West Creek
Just after midnight
As thousands slept
In the valley and neighborhoods below
Mostly unaware, what was to befall
As the firestorm mounted the ridge
And descended
We raced to alert friends, neighbors
We called
We texted
We ran
For the cars and trucks and SUVs
We safeguarded dogs
Horses and cats
Goats and sheep
Our moments would later
Seem an eternity
Time to grab a few items
From each home we ran
We escaped
Under the advancing ash
As winds powered an inferno
A descending blaze
We would soon realize
We were among the fortunate
Of what was about to explode

We were all running in the night
Some of us ran under sparks

And cinders alight
One visitor was wondrous
Could it be fireflies in the night?
Then quickly grasped
A stark realization of doom
Sweeping down with massive winds
A firestorm, advancing too soon
Down from the ridge above
Cascading into vineyards
Setting fields and forests a blaze
Furies of sparks igniting the way
Storm winds causing trees to buckle
Powerlines to sway
A deep and ominous roar
Homes erupted into flames
While that serpent orange glow
Advanced quickly
Massively
Swallowing all in its way
Igniting and taking down
Manzanitas and bays
The Buck Eyes in its path
But the big oaks stood fast
Knowing the Phoenix
Burned into their past
Deep in their roots

We were all running in the night
At 1:00am, we jumped into cars
Jumped into swimming pools
Retreated to wine cellars as a last stand

While the storm launched fireballs
And the front advanced
In our panic to escape
We drove through fences
Jumped curbs
Broke down gates
One hundred thousand of us
Ran to evacuate

We were all running in the night
We ran between the flames
Unaware that disaster had descended
Upon our doorstep unannounced
Until the final moment in the night,
When neighbors, strangers, firemen, police
Pounded at our doors, until we ran
Into the fires with fright
Sheriff's officers blinded
Drove through smoke and flames
Running home to home
Beating on doors
Calling out on loudspeakers
For people who still remained
Leave your homes!
You have to go now!
In the midst of flames
Mark West
Coffee Park
Fountain Grove
Rincon Ridge
Larkfield

Riebli
Redwood Road
Would be consumed that night
As tornados of flame spun aloft
And ripped down the hills
Obliterating everything in its path
Spiraling across a six lane freeway
Huge sections of the Hilton's roof
Lifted, twisted high overhead
Carried by tumultuous winds
Descending
Into the most unsuspecting of place
Consuming stores, restaurants
And homes in the night
Lifting cars off the ground
Sending burning timbers
Into a thermal upheaval
Floating in the sky for a mile
Descending into Coffey Park
1300 homes alight!
And still no emergency alert,
After four hours of blaze and fright
We could have had a better chance
Had they just had the courage
To press that button to let us know
That hell was coming from above

We were all running in the night
One person opened his front door
In Coffey Park
To see a thousand homes ablaze

He thought Pyongyang
Had launched a bomb
And sent the flames
As some of us ran from our homes
The winds slammed the door
Leaving our children locked inside
Hospitals were being evacuated
As the storm swept into the valley wide
As far as we could see
The city was burning in the night
How could we ever imagine
Wild fires chasing us from homes
Fires that had started five hours before
But the emergency alert lay silent
Before the storm's thrust
Wakened by neighbors and volunteers
And strangers who pounded on the doors
We ran in a moment's notice
No thought to save any item
Some of us wore just night clothes
Some of us ran barefoot in the streets
With nothing but skin and cloth
Some were on fire as we ran from the flame
Separated from our families, amid disarray
We ran naked along Mark West highway
Along burning streets, picked up by strangers
In our boxers and night robes
As the exodus of traffic
Slowed county roads

We were all running in the night

Some of us were trapped
Inside the flames
We were the 44
Who would fail to escape
And be remembered in later days
We were a family
Running along a forgotten road
In a valley in Mendocino
We were trapped inside our garages
In Redwood Valley and Fountain Grove
We were elderly for the most part
We hobbled with our canes
As our wife struggled to run away
We were 100 years old
Remembering battles of China
In another life that had been
We couldn't move so fast
Our cars careened off the road
Our wheelchairs couldn't roll
We went to sleep earlier than the rest
We were over 80 years old, struggling
As the fires erupted and enfolded
Where we stood, where we ran
In the end we were all
Running in the night

Exodus

We drove down the canyon

Into darkness

The fire was above us

Rendezvousing at a parking lot

With the dogs in our two cars

10 minutes down the line

Our initial flight

On Old Redwood Highway

At Molsberry's Market we met

More and more people

Pouring out of the hills

Trucks with trailers carting animals

Bags packed high

Pulling boats, campers

Cars filled with cats and dogs

Such as ours, barking and scared

We rallied around Molsberrys

An angel in a black four wheel drive

Handing out bottles of water

From the pickup bed of a truck

To stunned people

Wandering about

Trying to sort out

What was coming down

From the fires above

How could we know

In sixty minutes

There'd be a fire fight

Where we stood

Rincon Fire Department

Making an heroic stand
Larkfield would blow up that night
Hundreds of homes would go down
Most of us got out of Mark West alive
Walking around in some trance
In the parking lot, no plan
Futures unraveling
Met my neighbor, RJ
We embraced in the moment
No future
No past
No way
To understand
What's next
We watched his cell phone
A firey video emerged
Camera from his front porch live
Recording the violent torrent
Of sparks, cinders and fire
Swirling in hellish winds
Consuming the forest
His home in the midst
Only 10 minutes after we left
Our home was next
On the hillside
Trees swayed, manic
Everything burning in the night
Until the camera at his door
Melted and stopped
Freezing images of destruction
There'll be no going back

Geyserville Inn

Next thought

Survival

A place to stay

Geyserville Inn

Twenty miles away

It was 1:30am

When I dialed them

Reserved the last room

Said we had a small dog

I lied

Planned to sneak the bigger one

Inside

Be there within the hour

We set out driving north

Fires erupting in the hills

Swallowing everything

Fountain Grove ablaze

Larkfield would be next

Fires would jump six lanes

On Highway 101

No one

Could have imagined

Coffey Park incinerated

By a wildfire in the night

We just kept driving north

To the Inn

Checking in

To our one room

Right off the lobby

Said I'd forgot to mention

We have two dogs

And one of them is big

My eyes bleary

Manager looked at me

Said no worries

You're all right

He knew

We'd run

In the face of hell

Others coming now

Looking for shelter

As the Pocket Fire

Erupted across the river

Manager offered us a nod

We went to our room

It was about ten by twelve

Small window to the parking lot

With our paper bags, dogs

Cell phones had quit

No TV

No landline

No internet

Went outside

Watched the hills

Illuminate

As fires tumbled

From Mayacamas Ridge

Smoke permeating every breath

We were slowly surrendering

To a grim realization

Beginning to surround us

As we stood with the dogs
At the Geyserville Inn

Severed

Awake through the night

Trapped in replays

Bewilderment

Smoke hanging in the air

Constant reminder

Some sort of surreal

State of oblivion

Small dark hotel room

Dogs sleeping

We're constantly awake

Recounting

Unwinding

Severed

Lying in the dark

Always, the smoke

No communications

Rigorously

I rise before dawn

Go to the inn's lobby

Get a copy

Of the newspaper

Press Democrat

To read cover to cover

The only solid connection

To our previous world

Scale is starting to emerge

Names like Tubbs, Nuns, Atlas

Redwood, Pocket, lighting up the pages

A hundred thousand people displaced

300 missing
Everything still burning
Out of control
As the sun rose

Guests are changing at the inn
First morning the lobby was full
Of Europeans
Travelers
Tourists
People from faraway places
Checking out
Vacations Interrupted
Bags packed to leave
Fleeing
The onslaught of displacement
Options of new horizons to see
Then waves of locals
Checking in
From across the Russian River
Driven out by the Pocket Fire
They've got dogs and cats too
Barking and yowling in the rooms
The inn manager is juggling
Reservations against desperation
A large wedding party
Scheduled to arrive
Booked a year ahead
Family
Friends
Relatives

Coming in on flights
We all may have to give up our rooms
We reaffirm our place on a daily basis
They can't promise anything
But everyone accepts it graciously
No arrogance, because something
Overwhelming confronting us all
You just turn to faith and say
It will somehow work out

With the tourists gone
I feel like a foreigner from the south
Everyone in the inn is from Geyserville
The Pocket Fire
They all know each other
We're the only refugees from Tubbs Fire
20 miles down the road
Every morning over coffee and the PD
We piece together the mayhem
That first night I thought the fires
Were terrorism
So many all at once
But then it was revealed
Wind damaged power lines
Lit the sparks
We ask the front desk once again
Can we have the room for another night?
Or do we have to check out?
Each day we go to our friends
Connie and Rodney, in Cloverdale,
They welcome us and the dogs

We've know each other

Practically our whole lives

They offer us a place to stay

But we hold that as a last resort

They're allergic to dogs

But gracious

Got a reprieve on the fifth day

Manger said the wedding party

Cancelled reservations

They'd read the news

Didn't seem like the time

Or place to celebrate

New beginnings in the face

Of still roaring fires

Smoke and haze

And thousands displaced

Our room at the inn

Was extended a full week

Which made us feel joyous

At such a small thing

We got an upgrade

With a balcony

Facing east

We could see fires

Still burning in the night

Marching south

From Mercuryville

Toward River Rock Casino

We boiled water in the room

To pour in paper cups of oatmeal

We surveyed the dogs and paper bags

A few pieces of clothes
The room in disarray
I only owned about 20 things now
Couldn't find my glasses
Somehow misplaced
Where did the car key go?
Couldn't concentrate
Without the fire racing in
Fixating itself between
Everything I could see
We'd gather on the lawn
Let the dogs run
They didn't seem to care
That the hills were still ablaze
We stood in awe as a 747
Swept in to drop retardant
Saved a home, some vineyards
On the eastern hillside
Dozer crews started rolling in
Some stayed at the Geyserville Inn
Operator said they'd driven all night
They got the call in Southern Cal
We need 50 dozer crews now
He's been fighting fires since 1985
Said this is just the beginning
It was all sinking in

Crow's Nest (Dream)

I've climbed to the crow's nest
Sixty feet off the deck
The water is rough in the winds
The mast is pitching back and forth
Like a pendulum, in sweeping arcs
I hold on tight, watching the waters
Of the bay surrounding me
And the buildings that line the shores
A small sturdy steel vessel struggles
Against the wind and waves
Plunging beneath the surface
Bursting forth and pulling me forward
I'm watching for something
But I'm not sure what
I remember the wind
Gale like in its furry
I'm gripping the metal bar tight
It seemed like night
But the shore and buildings are visible
Then it appears
In the distance
Small at first
A wave
But it starts to build
Rising from the sea off the port bow
Massively
Other waves
Of equal magnitude
Emerging on the starboard side

They are steepening

Coming toward me

Building in size

Closing in

For a cataclysmic moment

Towering 100 feet

Then 200 feet and more

Cresting as they enter the bay

Buildings and beaches

Are being swallowed

By the onslaught of the waves

Turbulence descends

I quickly weigh my odds

Remain in the crow's nest?

Stay above the fray or bolt?

My adrenaline rushing

I felt the decision burst in my chest

As I raced down the mast

Ran to reach the deck

Of the steel vessel

Before the waves could arrive

And crush all in their way

Breakers fall in a thunderous roar

Over the shores and buildings below

I'm running on the steel deck

As a metal door swings open wide

An engineer steps from the bowels of the boat

Offering swift recognition

He looks like my neighbor RJ

Who texted me

That fires were coming down from the ridge

We both head for the pilot house
I turn a heavy bronze wheel
That opens the door
RJ and I enter
Inside four men stand around a dense array
Of valves, gauges, levers and instruments
The ferrous, engineered world of survivalists
They greet us solemnly with but a nod
Then continue plotting their course
As the giant waves break over the top
Of the steel vessel
Leaving destruction
In its wake

Fields of Gray

The worst part

In the early hours

Was the hope

That our home

Somehow, survived

You dream up scenarios

Clay, stucco, tile and cement

Bordered by a vineyard

Facing a firestorm

It would take a miracle

But we held onto hope

You cling to it

Like a life boat

After you've capsized

You search for reason

All the while

Running up and down

Mental

Emotional

Corridors

Cut off from the world

Calling out

Trying all the doors

Looking for answers

Friends drove us

To Mark West Springs Road

The next day

Smoke still hanging

Thick in the air

Traffic jams
Sheriff locked it down
Closed to those
Trying to return
Too dangerous
They rightly said
Searching for the missing
Clearing trees from roads
Shutting down live wires
In my mind I kept replaying
How the house might survive
For fires have whimsical ways
Maybe it didn't ignite
Clay, stucco, tile and cement
Bordered by a vineyard
But then the stories
Began to unfold
Staggered by the magnitude
The destruction, human toll
Bigger, than we ever imagined
Day two
TV news crew
Broadcasting live
On Crystal Drive
Videoed the end of our road
Our mailboxes stood untouched
The neighbor's fences solid
Trees with green leaves
Victor's two white pickups
Unscathed
Gave us hope

Clay, stucco, tile and cement

Bordered by a vineyard

Day three

Emboldened by the news

Two neighbors

Braved ash and fumes

With emergency responders

Made it to the neighborhood

Grim images of smoke

Wreckage

Transmitted back

At dusk

From a mobile device

Seven homes on our road

All confirmed, gone

But nobody could see our place

So we hoped

Clay, stucco, tile and cement

Bordered by a vineyard

Day five – RJ sent me a link

Said it didn't look good

New satellite images

Of the fire zone

Infrared photos

Exposed havoc and gloom

I clicked and traced

The Tubbs Fire realm

The road to our place

Scorched and burned

Through abstract colors

Red, was the green foliage

Not much of that

Black, charred remains

Of forest habitat

Gray, the ashen piles

Of homes and structures

Laid to waste

Dotted the valley and hillsides

Hundreds and hundreds

Gone

Only a few stood

Miraculous survivors

Like ghost ships

That weathered a storm

After the rest the fleet

Perished beneath the sea

I clicked our road

Adrenaline flowed

Found our home

Clay, stucco, tile and cement

Bordered by a vineyard

Enlarged the view

The image crashed in

Felt that final blow

Flattening hope

Our home among

The ashen

Fields of gray

She

She was burning
From the inside
I could feel her
Giving up her past
Creations, devotions
A quarter century
Slipping
From her grasp
All her passions
Entombed in the walls
As she relented
To the forces
Surrounding her
In the night
Crimson messengers
Darting in and out
Inflaming her soul
Telling her
To give up the fight
Relinquish her control
She tried to resist
Stoic to the end
But the heat
The flame
Was building
From within
I'll never know
Those final moments
The collapsing

Of her walls
When she succumbed
To the stress that befalls
Her dreams surrendered
An ecstasy crumbling
When her loved ones
Have left her alone
To face her demise

Chariste

We'll never forget you

We rescued you

A forlorn dog

From a remote corner

Of the world

Abandoned in the forests

Of Taiwan

And then

On board that China flight

Gliding into San Francisco

On a Tuesday night

You came to us

To a new world

You were strong

Determined

Carrying an intelligence

That stunned us

How I loved seeing you run

On the trails of our land

And through the vineyards

Of the Alexander Valley

Even, in the smoke

Of the Pocket Fire

After our exodus

You were so exuberant and happy

In your extraordinary strides

With total freedom

In a new world

You took control of the environment

Chased the deer from the gardens
With a passion you ran
Established a perimeter of safety
Stood watch at the entry ways
You studied the landscape
Could detect even slight change
Day to day
You were looking out
For us
I loved walking with you
You were the huntress
You owned the place
You owned our hearts
Then…that fateful night
I saw your fear
When the ash was drifting
Ahead of the flames
You sensed danger
In the smoke
As the fire descended
So quickly you surmised
The peril in the night
You and Jasper were first
Into the cars, the most precious
Days later…
After the hotel rooms
Living out of paper bags
Your energy boundless
Your confinement, wearing thin
We had to make that decision
To let you go…

Driving across the Golden Gate
Your head resting on my shoulder
I'll remember that feeling forever
Intently watching the multi-lanes
You trusted me
My hand at the wheel
You watched, the traffic
And interchange of humanity
You were fascinated, fixated
And we were brain dead
At the idea of giving you up
Just too much to bare
The lack of space, no future plan
After you had your run
On a place that had no end
Fence line to fence line
Every day, just letting your heart
Go wild into the hills of Sonoma
You were a free spirit
We couldn't see you tethered
Into an uncertain life
Surrounded
By limitations and confines
Hotel rooms, paper bags
Fenced in by uncertainty
Day to day
So with heavy heart
We were letting you go
But into what, we feared?
Driving up that unknown coastal road
Into Pacifica, a good reference from Tina

Delivering you into yet another home
On your life journey from across the seas
Your inquisitive trusting eyes
Searching for contact
Understanding
Your playfulness
Your intensity in the chase
No holding you back
Even when we delivered you
To this new home
You instantly made a new friend
And you ran and ran and ran
And played
Martina would care for you
You didn't notice us quietly leaving
Until later
She said you cried
But they loved you too
And the tears welled up
In our departure
But at least we knew
You were in a good place
Dammit to hell the firestorm
It took our love

The Ocean

For three weeks
We wander everyday
By the seaside
The smell of smoke
Haunting
Pure ocean breeze
Breakers roar
Drowning out memory
Of fire rising thunderous
Crashing over trees
Like waves over rocks
The roar of energy
Unleashed
But the ocean
Made us feel good
Water
As far as we could see
Reminding me
Where I grew up
On the Northcoast
At the edge of the sea
Eureka's Humboldt Bay

Can't shake that moment
Standing dumfounded
Before flames
Close to midnight
It just keeps playing
In my mind

I'm bewildered
Like I dreamt it
But didn't live it
Now I remember
Driving past
The inferno's face
Toward Calistoga
Just to see
The other side
Blood moon in smoke
Reappeared china white
Once past the front
I wondered what would be
If fire had leapt the road
Cut me off from our home
Before I could double back

Now
Walking along bluffs
Same canvas shoes
Black warmups
Blue GranFondo T-shirt
That I ran in that night
Haven't gotten around
To shopping yet
Friends gave me
Pants, a belt, a shirt
Like I'm on some vacation
Plane lost all my bags
Just walking the beach
From out of nowhere

Didn't plan this trip
But I'm on it
At the edge
Of the sea
Hole in my heart
Like a loved one died
I'm just moving forward
Along the path
Making strides
Looking out
Life suspended
Hoping to land
On my feet

Gone

Two weeks

After the fires

Hot zones contained

Roads to our home

Opened

We rolled through

Sheriff and police lines

National Guard posts

County Health Stations

We were given Tyvek suits

Booties, goggles, water bottles

For the trek back to our home

Fourteen days of media

Satellite images

Photographs

Of neighbor's

Burned properties

Prepared us

Hardened us

For what lay ahead

But nothing prepares you

For the scale of destruction

The miles and miles

Of burndown

In the wake of a Firestorm

Old Redwood Highway

We made the turn East

Flanked on both sides

By remains of Larkspur-Wikiup

Mark West and Sky Farm
Hundreds of homes flattened
Scorched earth
Charcoaled trees
Some down, some broken
Just about every home in sight
Gone
Power lines down, collapsed
As far as you can see
Just ash piles, debris heaps
Hundreds of car bodies
Blackened, abandoned
Gutted and already rusting
Towering brick chimneys
Like lone sentinels
Left in a war zone
Fracturing the horizon
Against a blue sky
Four miles of this
As we wound our way
Back home
Into Reibli Valley
Every home a landmark
Of memory on that drive
Now gone
Well-known places
Now looked unfamiliar
Places hidden by trees and foliage
Now revealed
Two homes survived
Pristine islands in the storm

Everything and every home around them

Gone

Even the home between the two homes

Gone

We entered our road

I felt the same chills

Like at midnight

Two weeks ago

Standing before

The Firestorm

The first four homes

On our road

Gone

The next two homes

Across the creek

Gone as well

We stopped at our drive

Walked up our lane

To the steel gate

Still locked in place

From our exit in haste

The gate motor, burned

Jasper stayed in the car

Sniffed the air

He used to jump from the car

And run to the front door

Now he was wary and overcome

By pungent scents

The sharp odor of destruction

We walked past

The locked steel gate

The burned down fences
Taking a side path
Some trees survived,
Others looked dead, opaque
Silhouettes of the past
Came to the John Deere
Skeleton in the driveway
Blown apart in the blast
Strange, no pain or remorse
Flaming out from our hearts
We coldly surveyed the scene
No sense of past or future
Minds blank in disbelief
Standing on the front steps
Of a once majestic home
That was now absolutely
Gone

Valeen (Dreams)

I'm riding a child's tricycle

Through the streets of Eureka

My home town

At 50 miles per hour

A cat on my lap

I think it was Mittens

Our family cat from the '50s

Peddling furiously to keep up

Passing all the cars

It took me over three blocks

Just to slow down

And not lose control

Maintaining perfect balance

The smell of burning rubber around me

Then I was at our property again

In the midst of its destruction

Everything in burned disarray

I needed to be at a community workshop

In Santa Rosa

To deal with the debris cleanup miles away

But I was far from that spot

I'd lost my phone and couldn't call

I needed a ride but had no money

Then I was on a boat

It was leaking, taking on water

It was Ernie Lampella's boat

From the 1970s on Humboldt Bay

The Valeen - his wife's name

They lived on the island

Where my grandmother had lived
In the early 1900s
But her house burned to the ground
A fire set by my father and me in 1958
It was a three-story Victorian
Abandoned and rickety
When we lit the match
We sat there and watched
The whole thing go up in smoke
The boat was leaking
Ernie wasn't alive anymore
Neither was my grandmother
But Ernie's boat was the only means
To get me to the fire and debris
Removal workshops
In Santa Rosa
I set sail and kept moving
Hoping to make it in time
I needed to clean up the mess

Fire Zombies I

At first, we appear normal

Then it starts

"Oh, you're one of them," he said

Immediately casting us into uncertain light

Something, like the walking dead

I think it's because we seem preoccupied

Bags piled in the car

Dog afraid to get out of the car

It's the only thing that still exists that he remembers

Besides his two zombie owners

Our eyes have that glazed appearance

Possessed from a primal experience

That makes us do strange things

Our language becomes disconnected

Words drift off course

Fire zombies show up on the wrong day

Give inaccurate information

In a state of oblivion

Fire zombie dogs will crap on the carpet

When all the doors are open and people around

Their total abandon lacks sense or time

But we weren't born this way

We were forged in a moment

When a storm descended into our lives

Disrupting our dreams and sense of time

When we abandoned place

Set out on a blind run

Into the night

Forcing us into the moment to confront ourselves

Establish a sense of real time

We attempt to deny but are forced to embrace

Fire zombies find refuge in a hotel room

And then in a distant seacoast town

To avoid the smoke

Once based in a sprawling house

Filled with generations of artifacts, history

Now they have seven paper bags

No home no place

Fire zombies are living in the car

It breeds spaciousness in the mind

A sense of letting things go

Despite trying to hold on

Zombies live in a state of conflict

Remembering the past

Vague in an empty chest

Navigating the present

Like that day at Bob Cat House

At Sea Ranch

On Sonoma Coast

Fire zombies prepared to check out

From the rental home

All that remained of their life's documents

Rendered into a single black business bag

Passports, computer, wallet and credit cards

Driver license, iPad, safe deposit keys and cash

Insurance documents, ID cards and bank passcodes

Vital phone numbers, storage keys, lock codes and more

That is the bag the zombies need to protect

At all cost to maintain what's left of sanity

It's all down to that

Fire zombies load the car and make one last check

Of the four-night rental home to make sure

They have everything safely aboard

They go meticulously room to room

Scan the house for any sign

Of what personal belongings

Might remain behind

They see only original contents of the home

They're satisfied, they're ready to go

Fire zombie dog is in the backseat

They drive down the coast and turn into the mountains

Zombies plan to meet the architect and get the plans

For the adjuster flying in from the east

"It's a beautiful day" one zombie says to the other

"Yes it is" the other answers

They drive through the coastal hills of Annapolis

Passed the vineyards and head for Dry Creek

50 miles of country road with no services or traffic

The road is narrow, steep and winding

With an occasional logging truck

Fire zombies don't care about those details

They are enjoying the countryside

And the simplicity of their new life

They are out of reach

Of cell phone coverage and like it

It makes them relax in the moment

Of the countryside and hills

An hour and a half later

Zombies reach Russian River Valley

Their phones regain connection

There is a message, they click the message.

"Mr. G, this is housekeeping at Bob Cat House.

You left your black bag on the dining room table.

With your hat

Should we send it to you?"

Zombies laugh at the message

Hah! Forgot the bag!

They call the number

But nobody has heard of the person

Who left the message

Zombies laugh again

Maybe this is the final straw

The final eradication of identity for zombies

Now it's just the car and the dog

And paper bags

The other dog's already gone

Zombies drive on and swear

They'll be back to get that bag

Fatal Night

I didn't get it at first

She was so ballistic

Like a sheet in the winds

Her home taken from her

Leaving only ashes

Without amends

She'd put her heart and soul

Into those embers that glowed

For a quarter century

Without end

All the art

The heirlooms

Antiques

The silver

Crystal glass

The linens

Vases

Old clocks

Remembering

Years before

She'd wept on the stairs

Of our first home sold

Up in the Northwest

She couldn't reconcile

Everything had a price

Even your domicile

She said you Americans

Sell everything with a smile

But my home is like a mother

Something I won't sacrifice
I didn't get it at first
Until that fatal night
When a lifetime of reflections
Disappeared in a flash of light

M5 Reckoning

We drove up and saw you

Standing by the tricked out

BMW M5 with four exhausts

The racing wheels, black paint

Aggressive stance as you waited

For us by the door

It was the only car in the lot

And you were there first

The insurance adjuster

Sent from the East

To determine our fate

In the aftermath of the storm

You didn't look me in the eye

When we shook hands

I knew what I was dealing with then

That this would be a physiological war

Your M5 with 600 horsepower

Against our 2.0 station wagon

In the diplomatic subtle form

We went into the meeting

I gave you all the information

The plans that you'd asked for

But I was caught a little off-guard

By your personal side

Likely, steeped in professionalism

From a corporate guide

We covered preliminary information

A few personal stories aside

But in the back of mind was that M5

Your power house, 11 seconds to 200 km/h
Hung in the breach
You'd come to meet us in your aggressive
Practiced ways, but I could see
Through all that
By the car of your choice that day
When all the pleasantries were said
There was nothing left to present
We stood and walked out of the meeting
Shook hands, without eye contact again
And I was waiting for you
To fire up that adrenaline machine
And wheel off to the next account
The next victim of your regime
But you just walked past that M5
Far across the parking lot
To a distant slot under a tree
Where you opened the door, quietly
To the smallest KIA that can be
And I felt totally absurd

Torn by the Wind (Dreams)

Last night in my sleep
I rode my bicycle to Seattle
I'd forgotten something
I don't remember what
But we used to live there
Couldn't remember why we'd left
My bicycle was electric
It was lightning fast
Went from Sonoma to Seattle
And back in a flash
State patrols couldn't see me
I was moving in another world
Trying to keep my grasp
As I got close to Sonoma
The highway disappeared
Only fragments
The closer I got to our home
The smaller the fragments
I had to slow down,
It was rough terrain
But the bike
Had a mind of its own
I held onto the bars
But was off the seat
Trailing behind,
Clinging, just holding on
The road finally crumbled
And just disappeared
But my bike was flying

Over large holes
Black landscape
Charred remains
Couldn't recognize the road
That used to lead me home
It was wild and primitive
So I just clung to the bars
For the ride
Doing pirouettes
Gliding through the air
Magical in the movements
I was an apparition
Looking for an imaginary home
That never would appear
Some sort of a memory that
Just carried me along
But the road home led nowhere
Leaving me just flapping
From the those bars
Like some sort of cloth
Torn by the winds

Fire Zombies II

Fire zombies go to a Chinese restaurant for lunch
After lunch they go to the car
But Zombie Dog has snuck into the front seat
He's a dachshund, a rescue dog from Spokane
Found abandoned in a parking lot
He wasn't always a zombie dog
But the fire was the final straw
He ran to the car and sat shivering in the front seat
He doesn't like change, it scares him
Zombie Dog can't go for walks anymore
He only wants to be in the car
It's the one familiar thing left
His new bed is in the backseat
He spends a lot of time in that bed
After moving into our fifth house
In the first two weeks after the fire
Zombie Dog liked the car the best
Now he'd snuck into the front seat
That's where we found him
After Chinese food
I set my phone on the top of the car
And picked up Zombie Dog
Placed him in the back seat
We had a piece of chicken for him
He was pleased, we drove away
Talking about what we do next
Negotiated traffic through Windsor
Then we slowed down
At a busy intersection

My iPhone slowly slipped off

The roof of the car

And down the windshield

I was glad it had the rubber case

That slowed it down

Zombie brain thought

Turn on the windshield wipers

Get rid of the phone

It's a fucking nuisance

Zombie phone had photographic records

Of the content of our home

For the insurance adjuster

Family photos, friends' addresses

Our music collection

I stop the car in traffic and get out

I don't pay attention to a car honking

Zombies don't feel pressure

I retrieve the iPhone

From the hood of the car

We drive away

Laughing

But underneath it all

I know I'm losing it

And the Angels Came Knocking

With folded wings
They came silently
Knocking on the door
After midnight
It's time to depart
They whispered
You must go swiftly
Leave all behind
Place your faith
In one another
And with those
Whom you trust
For all that stands
Before you
Will soon be rendered
To ash

Into the valley
And darkness we went
No plan, no destination
Or intention
We found a country inn
Lit up in the night
The fluttering of a wing
Offering us respite
They welcomed us
And our two dogs
The last room in the inn
Would be ours

From the valley we watched
The glowing hills
As the fires spread
Down from above
Wondering what would befall
Our home
And as I stood in the darkness
By the car
At 4:30am
Listening to song
Smoke drifting in the air
'Three Little Birds' floated by
The voice of Bob Marley
Singing, "Don't worry about a thing
Cause every little thing
Gonna be alright"
And I felt chills
From that music
Carried by angels
Before the dawn

And the angels came knocking
Friends, welcomed us
Invitations arrived
Saying you're not alone
From San Francisco, Ashland and Maine
Humboldt, Seattle, Half Moon Bay
And from the Russian River Valley
We went to the sea
Walked the shores
Rejuvenated

By salt air to breathe
Strangers
From the seaside town
Came to our door
With food and wine
Welcoming us
From our plight
To their remote coastal home
Embracing us
In their grace

And the angels came knocking
Three more arrived
Finding us a home
In the countryside
High upon a coastal ridge
We looked out over hills
And farms
To Point Reyes and south
Hawks drifted like kites
In the dawn
As far as one could see
Grasslands
Dotted with cattle and sheep
Ships emerged and disappeared
On the horizon of the Pacific
Beneath vapor trails
Soaring endlessly
Our displacement vanquished
Into reflections sublime
Though as holidays approached

Our hearts remained empty
We couldn't embrace the cheer

And the angels came knocking
Once again
This time a small packet
Left at the door from New York
To our temporary home
On Western shore
It was a message
Affirming a shared 15 years
A Christmas ornament
A thoughtful card
Then, many more knocks
Came to the door
The fluttering of wings
Packets piled up
Cards and ornaments
From distant place
The State of Texas
A Lake Placid bear on skates
They sent traditions
Ornaments from collections
Some with stories
Some with personal reflections
There was a Glass Ball
With us painted in the midst
Shaman's Leather
A Sail Boat
Wyoming prints
They came from Nantucket

Wisconsin and abroad
Sequined Lobsters
A Czech doll
A Moravian star

And the angels still kept knocking
A Glass Candy Cane from London
A Big Apple on the tree
Snowflakes
Swedish Tomte
A Heart from Willamette
Red Currants
A Polish figurine
Each one flying in
From a special place
Scattered across maps
Of origin they came
From overseas
Deserts and Great Plains
Each one wrapped for flight
Bearing a special individual's light
Inspired by an angel
From the mountains
Of Wyoming
They all joined to adorn
Our holiday tree in the end
And on the Solstice
We gave thanks for such gifts
And for the angels
That came knocking
On our doors in the night

Aftermath

In the end, it took 11,000 fire fighters, some from other states and countries, and hundreds of dozers, trucks, helicopters and air tankers to put down the North Bay Firestorms in October 2017. Over 200,000 acres burned during the outbreak. Crews fought the blazes for weeks before finally containing them. Nearly 100,000 people were evacuated in the early hours of the fires that would consume over 7,000 homes and businesses. Forty-four people would perish that night across five counties and nearly 20,000 would be homeless as a result of the firestorms. Seventeen different fires were reported at once across the region, sparked by drought and wind-ravaged powerlines. Three days after the fires erupted, a plume of smoke spread nearly 100 miles over the state, with Napa Valley registering the worst air quality in the nation. San Francisco International Airport canceled over 250 flights due to low visibility.

The Tubbs Firestorm became one of the most destructive fires in California history. It took out over 5,600 structures in just a few hours, mostly homes. It burned over 36,000 acres, and 22 people died in the blaze that night as thousands evacuated. Other fires were equally devastating in Mendocino, Napa, Solano, Yuba and Lake Counties – the Nuns Fire, Atlas Fire, Redwood Valley Complex Fire, Sulfur Fire, Cascade Fire and Pocket Fire burned over 2300 homes and another 22 people perished in their wake.

Ironically, the October 8 Northern California Firestorms coincided with another deadly night of fire in American history when the "The Great Chicago Fire" exploded on October 8 in 1871, claiming over 300 people. On that same day and night, major wildfires erupted in Peshtigo, Wisconsin and parts of Michigan. The Peshtigo Firestorm would become the deadliest wildfire in American history claiming 1500-2500 people, burning over one million acres. Those historic October 8th fires were also fanned by massive winds.

In Sonoma, the rains returned about two weeks after the firestorm. People would have to wait before the Sheriff and National Guard al-

lowed them to return to their homes as emergency responders looked for missing persons, which totaled nearly 300 at one point, repaired downed power lines, removed fallen trees from roadways and contained gas leaks. In the weeks that followed, people slowly went back to their properties to find what little remained.

Second Fire

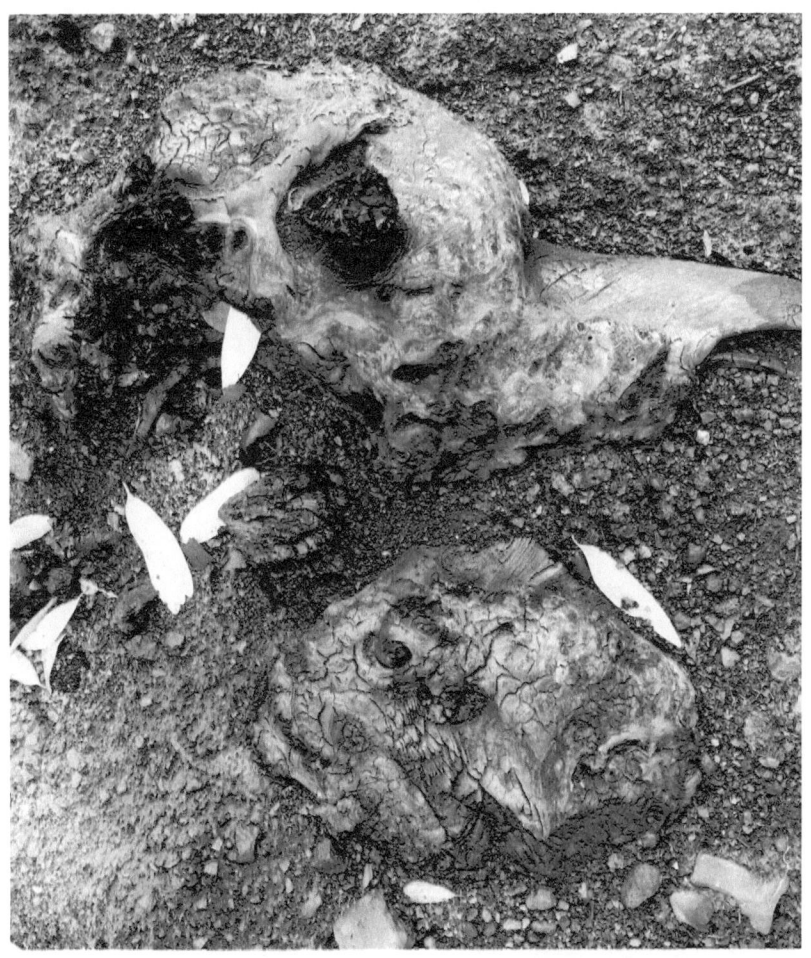

Second Fire

The Second Fire
Worse than the first
Premeditated like a curse
Arson you might say
Coming with cold flame
Icy to the touch
No wind, no oxygen
No scorching heat
Licking your soul
Burning from within
Touching your skin
A fire designed
To suffocate
While you're awake
Burn us in our sleep
Leave us weary
At sunrise
Their fire was not
A wild and raging spirit
Burning everything
In sight
In an unpredictable path
Renewing life in its wake
Theirs was a different fire
Personal
Designed to consume
And weaken from within
Their fire forces you
To place a value
On the spirit, the home

On dreams that come

In the night or the day

That's where they light the match

Ignite that icy flame

Flickering

Then unstoppable

Though bearable at first

But after weeks and months

As it smolders within

Like the oaks that burned

More than a hundred hours

Deep in the core

Leaving a hole in the earth

A hole in our heart

Their fire

Works the same way

Coursing through veins

Conjuring memories of where

All things lie tormenting

Until we give up our life

Downtrodden

In the moment

Burned out

But not afraid to fight

Their flames came cold

From the center

Of an insurance domain

Licking on the shores

Of our dignity

To stand up against

The second fire's roar

Night Hours

I feel better now

When I'm drinking

Forgetting it all

Can't wait till

The five o'clock hour

Drop my guard

Professional face

Sink into the view

Up here on The Ridge

Wine runs the course

Phone dead silent

Maybe awkward to call

After the burn down

Like that was our fault

Our sum total in the ash

They're afraid

I hear it in their voices

What's on the other end?

What if there's no cash?

Maybe despair or anguish?

Isolation settles

In the night hours

After bottles ring empty

Conversations hollow

Reasons to persevere

Crumpled by the wayside

When the answers appear

On distant islands

In another hemisphere

Imagining the flight
From it all
Then like yesterday
We stepped into a place
The fire spared
One of those islands
In the storm
Drew us hard
To contemplate
To buy that place
But it wasn't right
And we knew it
We were rushing in
Just to own a home
Be back in a place
Where we could function
Imagine the future
Once again
Not be trapped by this
Unearthed sensation
Losing all sense of place
And connections

Demons Between Us

Now you are seeing things
In the night
Flying over the house
Smoke in the air
Fires coming in your mind
Casting you in fright
You are outside in the dark
Looking for flames
You haven't slept in weeks
It's tearing you up
Though it's been six weeks
Since the fire's died
You are living miles away
From all that disarray
And I'm taking pills
To sleep through the night
When we ran from our dreams
Full throttle redlining
Drinking bottles of wine
To forget and move on
Now I'm in Texas
Hearing about androids
Hovering over the house
You're ready to run again
With the one-eared dog
To an imaginary place
Because nothing is safe
In our minds anymore
You on The Ridge

Me 1500 miles to the southeast
In a Galleria high-rise
Ready to throw my hands up and cry
What can I do at this hour so far away?
I have my own demons to fight
My own insomnia to slay
Even the dreams are catching up
Friends telling me in the night to beware
You're losing your place in this life
Which you'd carved out of stone
Now eroding to dust in the winds
Because you have no home
No place to go

Opt Out

The County laid it down hard

After the fires were out

Gave us six months

To clean the mess up

The ruins of our lives

They said opt in or opt out

That was their ultimatum

Go with the EPA and the Army Corps

Or find a private contractor

County said Army Corps was free

But that was half-truth, half-lie

We heard some Lake County stories

About people getting shafted by the Corps

Insurance drained, people in uproar

Properties maimed

Over-excavated

Paid by the ton

Bad communications blamed

But thousands of us had to decide

Which way was right, which way wrong

Went to town hall meetings

Neighborhood sessions

Scanned local firestorm networks

Read the Press Democrat

Nobody had hard answers

Though deadlines loomed

While underneath it all we understood

The need to clear the wreckage

From neighborhoods

Talked to the County

The Army Corps

Contractors

Adjusters

Architects

Nothing was for sure

Left me spinning

With vague notions what to do?

Thousands of dollars in question at stake

Serendipitously

Met a state emergency services lawyer

Thirty minutes before

The end of the final opt in day

He said opt in now, opt out later

It'll give you more time

So I went with the Corps

Got me off the hook

Hundred days down the line

Army scout called

Surveyed our site

Said they're coming

With the machines

Stand by, you'll be notified

Got the call

Went to property

An hour away

Waited two hours

Nobody showed

Went back home

Four hours from my day

Next day, got the same call

Did the same routine

Nobody showed again

Day three was a repeat

So I called Army Corps

They didn't know anything

Just a call center

No link

No clue

No person who knew

Called the Army Corps scout

She couldn't remember me

Or what property

The question was about

She wanted to link me up

With some firm

From back East

That was it

Done with this shit

Called the adjuster

Pressed him on funds

Said what I'd heard

On fire insurance networks

There was more money to be had

He admitted more money

Than at first

Ran to the County offices

Minutes before

They locked the door

Opted out on the Army Corps

Iced a debris cleanup deal

With a local engineer
And a contractor
Who lived down the road
Lost his family home
His machines burned
Gladly went with Alan
Trusted him
Opting out in the end
Locking the gate
To block the Army Corps
From coming in
At the final hour
Pandemonium

Failure

I keep thinking I'll get over it

But every time

I see an article published

On the failure

To use the county's

Emergency warning system

During the firestorms

And their choice

To remain silent

For weeks

I get agitated

We figured out the fire

At midnight

With our neighbors

We all fled minutes before

Our homes burned

To the ground

I will never accept

Their decision

Not to broadcast

They never even discussed

Using the system

"Based on policy"

They said it was more suitable

For hurricanes and tornados

Cited limitations of 90-character text

Fear of mass evacuations

Traffic jams

Again, I woke at 2am

First thing in my head

"Wildfires in eastern hills;

Be prepared,

Tune into broadcasts!"

Wrote it in two minutes

Less than 90 characters

How hard could it be?

They were bound

By uncertainty

Ineptitude

They didn't even know

How the system worked

Couldn't react

And so

The silence spread

As an ominous absence

Of warning

They had their historic chance

And failed

So shut them down

Hand over their office

To the sheriff's command

They were among the ones

That took decisive action

In the face of sudden

Overpowering destruction

They had limited communication

Quickly overrun

Hundreds of calls into 911

Lake County Sheriff

Took decisive action

Sonoma sheriff
Left the desk
Drove into the fire
Issued Nixle alerts
Updating outbreaks
Evacuation zones
Citizens
Police
Fire fighters
Ran door to door
Made it up on the run
They all took action
Sonoma Emergency Services
Maintained, silence
Before the storm

Battle of Vinograd

We were fighting

Room to room

House to house

In the neighborhoods

In the ashes and ruins

Behind burned-out foundations

Defending our homeland

Our heirlooms and art

Our families

From an army of adjusters

Descending from the East

Demanding line item accounts

Of our lives and memories

To be entered on spreadsheets

Their estimators against our recollections

Their algorithms against our receipts

Most which burned in the wildfire

On that Sunday eve

Their Wehrmacht against our belief

They had air power, with satellites

Taking Exactimate imagery of how we lived

To assess us and be used against us

When those terrible hours came

We had neighborhood groups

Friends and networks in the midst

Loose affiliations of modern time

To go against their machines

Massing behind the lines

Then their shock troops flew in

We were put under lamps scrutinized
How were our homes constructed?
When did we acquire that heirloom?
Keel-hauled through ashes
Time again
We fought them
On Rincon Ridge
Parker Hill
San Miguel Road
We fought them
Room to room
House to house
In the neighborhoods
In the ashes and ruins
Behind burned out foundations
Defending our homeland
Our heirlooms and art
Our families
From an army of adjusters
Descending from the East

Sister Cities

We're sister cities Houston
You and me
Even though
I'm a wine country town
Laid back in the rolling
California hills
Among the oaks
And you a sprawling
Energy giant
Dominating
A monotonous flat land
Your toe in the calm
Warm Gulf waters
My hand on the frigid
Wild Pacific shore
We're sister cities Houston
You and me
We've been through it all
In our own separate ways
Just weeks apart
Harvey for you
Tubbs for me
We couldn't be more different
Yet we are so much the same
When I sit in your cafes
In the Galleria, the River Oaks
Talk with people from your streets
It's like our streets our stories
Our cafés

Shared much the same way
From Cloverdale to Calistoga
Sebastopol to Santa Rosa
We're both survivors
We fight back against the odds
That come with the wind
We're sister cities Houston
You and me
You have your hurricanes and rain
We have our firestorms in the night
But our truths are linked
By an inseparable bond
That knows true loss
The abandonment of home
Incessant knocking on the doors
By strangers sent to rescue us
Now beloved friends
15 minutes to gather family
Pets and a few odds and ends
Then we run to the cars
On the streets of Houston
The valley roads of Santa Rosa
Leaving our dreams behind
And the demise unfolds
We're sister cities Houston
You and me

Sue the Winds

So you're going to sue the wind?

The winds of the Caribbean

The winds of Florida

The winds of Houston

The winds of Sonoma

Napa, Mendocino

Lake County

Southern California

The Carolinas

Maybe a Class Action?

Who did it?

The winds did it!

So sue the wind!

We'll sue the island of Tortola

While we're at it

For getting in the way

Of the winds!

Puerto Rico

Few lights to this day

Their schools in disarray

And with the winds

Fly in the lawyers

Layers of blame

To stalk the crisis

Forty percent to gain

In humanity's name

Cast the net, sow ferment

Hand out torches and pitchforks

To the crowd that gathers

In their square
As they chant – "Sue the winds!"
With banners a blaze
Marching toward
Golden ways

Spreadsheets

Flying in from Mumbai, Beijing or Tokyo
Not that big a deal
One to two days to acclimate
Moscow, Paris or London
Easier
Buenos Aires, Santiago or Rio
North south, no problem
But fire lag
Worse than jet lag
Taking us months
Filling out spread sheets
As I toss and turn
Waking at 1:20am
Every night, precisely
When our neighborhood was alight
I wake and start thinking, how we ran
What if we hadn't run?
What if we hadn't known what was coming?
What if I wasn't home, my wife alone?
If the dogs had run away
Before the flames?
Like that man down the road
Somebody had locked the steel gate
Fires all around
His dog perished in the blaze
As they tried to escape
I think about that
For a couple hours
At night when awake

Then fall asleep again

But it's a false sleep

Hollow

Waking at 3:40am

Wondering when this will end?

This goes on for months

Now a New Year – 2018

Drinking a bottle of wine every night

But that gives me no relief

Even after 90 days and seven cases

Throw in some tequila on the top

A few dozen beers and some pot

I've got a life and a job in the midst

Trying to shut down my mind

Double up on Ambien

Pressing the pharmacy to refill

Prescription that was consumed

But they are vigilant

Forcing me to wait until the date

I can buy it again

I just want to sleep

Forget the mayhem

Stop the storm

Clouding my head

Adjusters from the East

Demanding spreadsheets

Telling us to recite every item

From 30 years of our life

In every room and every drawer

Forcing us to remember

All that burned in the night

One item at a time
Like some sort of torture
Waterboarding effect
Forcing my head back into the ash
See what I can recollect
To salvage some more cash
Trying to make me give it up
They don't want to pay their share
So I lie awake at 5:15am
Thinking about that drawer
Remembering all that's within
Our home, the office, out in the yard
The kitchen, the guest room and garage
Every screw, toothbrush and light switch
Roll of tape, gloves, John Deere trailer hitch
And they want me to write all that down
In their spread sheet
Tell them when I bought those vise grips
The antiques, that bag of beans and the chips
And how much it would cost to replace?
That 1865 landscape
Hanging above our fireplace
Painted by a Civil War officer
Who'd managed to escape
A prisoner of war camp
How's that fit into a spreadsheet?
They're trying to burn me down,
Buy some time, place their cash
To mitigate their loss
And keep us tied up in our grief

Tossing and turning
Between their spread sheets

Hail Mary

It came out of nowhere

Like the wild winds of the east

As the sun set in the west

I heard the first chair sailing by

Whirling through the air

A guttural scream from deep

Wafted from a recess of pain

And bewilderment in the midst

That such a situation could befall

Lit up by the flames of alcohol

Fanned by the utter sense

Of the loss of it all

Second chair went twirling by

Much like the first, but farther

A higher arc, more velocity

More resolute, a deeper anger

Aimed at the hopelessness

The repulsive

Sedentary state of being

That we'd descended into

Provoking the rage

Then a third chair

This one a Hail Mary

From the deck

Spinning, arcing over the lawn

Into the bush by the trees

The screams for vengeance

Striking the Army Corps
They were coming
With machines to dig a hole
Where a heart once stood
To take the tree and her children
The last vestiges of spirit
As we spun and lay in a heap
For one last primal scream
For the pain and loss
That destroyed the dream

Zombies in the Kitchen

Arguing about everything

That's what zombies do

Doesn't take much

Couple bottles of wine

Not much sleep

Late night

Everything's fair game

Could be about the weather

Relatives, friends

Insurance, healthcare

Anything at all

One zombie got new slippers

All the other slippers burned

With the house

Art Zombie wanted to make a point

Held up the old slipper

With holes in its toe

To the million dollar

Rental house wall

Butcher knife in hand

Eyes a blaze

Jammed the blade

Through the slipper

Stuck it to the wall

Stepped back

Blade quivering

Admiring the image

It looked like still life

Next to the oil painting

Of an old country house

It just hung there

Butcher knife through a slipper

Stuck to the wall

Beautifully making sense

Fire zombies didn't have a house

They didn't give a shit

What the fuck are you doing?

Yelled the Practical Zombie

That wasn't their house

Practical Zombie thought

Security deposit!

Zombie with the knife

Thought art statement

Anger release

Became agitated

Art Zombie with

Alcohol eyes

One slipper on

One off

Pulled the knife from the wall

Screamed – are you insane?

Practical Zombie shut up

Didn't know the answer

That was the worst part

Up In the Air

I feel dizzy these days

Like a bird circling and circling

Looking for a place to land

But it's all discombobulated

Never had a use for that word

Until now

Some recollections of home

Intangible, an imaginary place

Like I dreamed it in a chaotic state

Awake, at 1:40am again

Head spinning

Tumbling in the winds

Always the winds

I'm lying awake

Wondering about the owls

They were in the trees last night

Calling out at the crescent moon

Tonight, they've gone silent

Holding on in the gale winds

Hunkered down, talons on a limb

I Google Earth

Zoom into Mongolia

Ulaanbaator - it's 2:00am

I'm planning a bike trek there

How many miles from Beijing I click?

Insomnia

Sending me down tributaries

Of curiosity

To places I dream

But our home address

Pops up instead

So I zoom in

To look from above

Thinking original images

May have withstood

The October fires

And mayhem

But it's just a pile of ash

Enshrined in Google Zoom

I zoom out

To our neighbor's home

All gone too

Seems virtual

Looking at devastation

From so many miles up

A glimpse of our life

But yet a short time ago

It was green gardens

A saltwater pool

Vineyards all around

I click back to Ulaanbaator

And wonder if they have firestorms

Though dust storms for sure

Always a price to pay

3:10am

Remembered my book plates

Years to write and contemplate

Just seconds to disintegrate

And now in the swirling ash they lie

Burned inspirations of a lifetime

Then there's the sound of coyotes again
Shrill sounds cutting through gale winds
And in the valley below I think of the Angus
Wandering in total darkness alone
What do they think about at 3:20am?
When rain pours down, winds blow
I stare at the ceiling in the dark
Imagining walls ablaze
Consuming antiques and artwork
All the things we loved and saved
As the clock moves on to 4:00am

I know all this will one day end
I'm trying to imagine
Where we'll live
With 90 days to go
Here on The Ridge
We'll go somewhere
Not imagined yet
As we're in the eye
Of the storm
Our raft adrift
Circling in the winds
No sail, no rudder
An open horizon
Riding the currents
Now 5:05am
I click into Kenojuak
Her natural realm
Her printed visions
From Cape Dorset

Turned to dust

Lost under a collapsed roof

But still

Alive in my memory

As I'm surrounded

By her owls

Calling in the woods

Hooting in the night

Can't go back to sleep

Alarm's set for 5:30am

When it goes off, I'll jump

Dress and grab packed bags

Step outside into the storm

And in the dark

Drive away

To the county airport

For a flight to the Midwest

And as the plane lifts off

I look east at sunrise

To the burned hills

Of Mark West Springs

Remembering

Our life

Among the oaks

The creeks

Manzanitas and bays

Before the storm

Swept time away

Just memories now

A false sense of place

Stares me in the face

From a reflection

In the plane window

Discombobulates

There's that word again

Now, I'm drifting in clouds

In a distant space

Jet engines roar

Looking down

At valleys and shore

Relinquishing my past

Rain pouring down

On the ruins

Of our home

Dissolving

Into the ground

As I fly away

Beyond All Logic

My neighbor Bob

Told me about the Hanley Fire

It burned the same path as Tubbs

In 1964

He'd lived on the road

The longest

Then I read about the Hanley Fire

Took three days

To get to Santa Rosa from Calistoga

Took out Fountain Grove

But there were fewer homes

Back then

Saw it in burned stumps

On our property

Scarred terrain

Subtle in undergrowth

Half a century later

But I always knew

It could happen again

After Lake County burned

I felt lucky to be living

Two ridges to the west

But it didn't escape me

Sometimes imagining

The hillside ablaze

During the day

Never the night

But in my mind

I was convinced

Air tankers

Smoke jumpers

Helicopters

Radios

Dozer crews

Fire brigades

Emergency warning

Would all step in

Save the day

Stop calamity

In a modern age

"It couldn't happen here"

Sinclair Lewis once said

Though I never considered

A storm in the dead of night

With lightning speeds

That defied all reason

Descending and obliterating

Everything in sight

Before sunrise

It was – beyond all logic

Now six months displaced

From fires, charred landscape

Idealistic ashes in the landfill

A circumstance

Erupts in southern latitudes

Touching people I'd met

Reflecting, that you can't escape

The most unsuspecting of fates

Like back on November 8th

2016

Far to the south
In Uruguay, near Paysandu
With friends on a farm
Late at night
Under a galaxy of stars
A thousand crickets
Frogs in serenade
On the Argentine frontier
Near a quiet farm town
Called Quebracho
Far from the fray
It was at ease out there
The world passing by
Unannounced
While the US election
Thundered to the north

In the days after the fires
I thought about that quiet
About that tranquil peace
Maybe we'd go back
For a couple weeks
To an open invitation
To stay on the farm
Let the world pass us by
For some time
Rejuvenate
In quiet countryside

But clouds vanished
In the Southern Hemisphere

Dryness set in
The region was parched
The worst drought to befall
South American history
Had engulfed the farm
The biggest natural disaster
In the world so far
In 2018
Global Warming
Spreading its wings
Crops wilted, animals stumbled
Distress descended on towns
Then a spurned lover
Started shooting people
On that quiet country road
Burned the neighbor's farm
To the ground
A young policeman
The mother-in-law
Dead in his wake
From a hell-bent rage
In the midst of drought
Writing his last testament
On that quiet country road
Apologizing to all
From a little schoolhouse
We used to drive by
On the way to the farm
Far removed
From the world
But nonetheless

Confused
A single shot
Rang out
Self-inflicted
A silent cry
Beyond all logic

Redemption

At times

I feel redeemed

In the whole burn-down

Freed from the legacies

The material entrapment

That surrounded my life

Absolute loss of possessions

Accumulated over a lifetime

Like the century-old typewriter

My grandmother's inlaid music box

My great-grandfather's redwood chest

Handed down

From generations

Things that I loved and valued

Gave meaning in my life

Hundreds of books read

Traveled with me for decades

Like friends, waiting on the shelf

Stories of values and imagination

Intrigue and despair, enlightenment

Adventures, histories, reflections of my life

Gone in the ashes

With the art, the embodiment of spirit and landscape

From Europe, America and First Nations

Scores of pieces adorning the walls

The tools of my father passed along

Waiting for a project to unfold and embrace

My guitars from 35 years ago

Traveling with me on the road

The emerald green Stratocaster

Playing the clubs and concerts

Across the Northwest

The howling crowds

The memories

The times

And I feel good

That all those things are freed

And I am freed with them

Captivity by material means

Friends ask, what about your ancestors'

Antiques, lamps and dishes lost?

From another time

Never to be replaced

Instruments a century old

What about the loss of place?

These circle my mind at times

Late into the night

And it's a death of sorts

Like losing someone you love

My mother – two years before

At 100 years old

Left a vacuum in my life

But I know

You can never own

Time

So I try to cherish and remember

What was shared along time's way

With the people and the things I loved

You carry it like a native language in your heart

To the ends of the earth until death do you part

Yes, we avoided destruction as it rained down
Coming to redeem captive energy
In hills, forests and the countryside
Our cities, our homes
Our lives
Though I will forever feel among the fortunate
From that fateful October eve
As we only lost
Material life

The Cloud

When it's swept away

Music, imagery pervades

Pulled down

From the cloud

Reuniting us with all

Sounds and moments

We loved, reflected amidst

Giving us connection

To places

Giving us a glimmer

Of the world we knew

Struggling to comprehend

A new world before us

Dislodged

All we remembered

Wiped away

Challenging us

To embrace

The next chapter

We click into the realm

Cloud timelessness

Amidst the words

And the sounds

The profound

The imagery

That survived

Resonates

From times past

Giving us substance

In the midst

Of chaos

Displacement

A new time

When people find

Opportunity

In this horrendous

Transgression

Upending our lives

Sending us down

Hollow pursuits

Insurance claims

Building permits

All a mirage

Friends disappear

Meanwhile

We're anchored

In the cloud

Jasper in a Clock (Dreams)

Time had come to a standstill
We're sitting by the roadside
At an outdoor restaurant
Jasper, the dachshund is there too
My grandmother's 19th century French clock
Is sitting on the table at the restaurant as we eat
We saved that old clock from the fire
Now it's on the table between us
Jasper crawls inside the clock
He's scared in strange places these days
His home is gone, so he seeks
Tight places, small passageways
Somehow he's gotten into the clock
His face is the face of the clock
The waiter comes with a pressurized
Italian coffee device strapped on his back
It's our vacuum cleaner that burned
With the house
But filled with espresso
He fills my cup
But the dog wants some too
The waiter pumps espresso into the clock
I see the clock walls bulge and urge him to stop
Opening the back door Jasper is huge
Filled with coffee and bulging
Up against the clock walls
The chimes and the pendulum
Will never work
So time just stands still

Corner Stones

They're digging up the foundation

Three excavators go after

Stem walls

Massive footings

Pilings sunk deep

Slabs of concrete

Twisted steel

Rebar

Digging out

The remains

Of what once was

The bedrock

Of our home

Meant to last

A century more

At least

So premature

With every scoop

They started with the roof

And the walls

Separated the steel

Ten truckloads in all

Then came the ash

The final renderings

Of all things past

Burned to fine dust

The grand piano frame

Sticking out of wreckage

Like an iron iceberg

Strings still attached
Turning to rust
My mother's Limoges set
Surfaces amidst the ruble
Another 10 truckloads
Of our past
Then to the foundation

I'm calm
Watching them chisel
Into the underbelly
Of what used to be our home
Pneumatic hammering
Splitting the slabs
Upending the pilings
Splitting our lives
Our connections
To this place
The reverberations
As diesel power
Digs into the earth
I feel the tremors
Through the souls of my feet
Where I stand and witness
The takedown
Of our home
Then 30 more truckloads
Of concrete
Reinforcement steel
300 tons
Unearthed

Hauled away

Ground up

Recycled

Stunning

The mass of it all

So deeply rooted

But momentary in the end

I really did feel rooted here

My grandfather Humboldt

My great grandfather Leroy

Buried just over The Ridge

In St Helena

From a distant time

And now in the aftermath

It all unwinds

And here I thought

Cornerstones

Were here to stay

But they were just

Temporary

The Stars

Venus

Always there first

Looking out to you

For solace in the storm

Every night, you are there

Steadfast in your realm

Brilliance in respite

Of all that unfolds

In this unraveling world

You are a beacon of hope

When all around me falls

Into confusion and betrayal

The ultimate denial of it all

But you give me hope

Effervescence in its wake

Something beyond my reach

To partake

Then I see Orion's Belt

Circling in the galaxy above

Every night

East to West

Giving me solace

That there is a rhythm

To it all in the end

Despite the fires

The breakups

The daily insanity

That knows no end

I used to sleep on the terrace

At our home, lie awake

On the summer nights

Study the stars

The moon

Little did I know

How fragile

Permanence could be

And now I'm out on another ridge

Looking over valleys

Watching the night sky

Counting the stars

In Orion's Belt

Suspended

Owls hooting their mantras

Telling me that everything's

Going to be alright

On this starlit

Winter's night

Regeneration

Regeneration

Back at our property

The home is gone

Just a vacant

Piece of earth

Laid bare

Surrounded by grass

And wildflowers now

Bursting out

California poppies

Everywhere

Grasses rejuvenated

Five and six feet tall

The birds are back

Bees are in the hollow

Of the old oak tree

Up on the hill

Just like before

Frogs moved into the pool

Saw a fox and deer

The fence is almost restored

The new well will be restarted

When electricity returns

Finished our spreadsheets

After six months of recall

Made an offer

On a home today

But it was passed over

Owners want a fire bonus

We're in an easy place

We decided not to participate

Let the house go

We feel good in the mornings

Still working on the evenings

No home in sight yet

The insurance company

Still dragging their feet

But it will come

So we are still renting

Out here on The Ridge

Where the horizons

Have no end

Landscapes

Its rejuvenating

To be on The Ridge

Months after the burn

Hundreds of feet

Above sea level

Looking southwest

Ships on the horizon

Aura of the Bay Cities

Illuminating the night

Undulating landscapes

Poking out of the valley fog

At Fallon and Two Rocks

Estero Americano Estuary

Glistens in the valley

Under afternoon sun rays

Barns with red roofs

White farm houses

Cattle herds

Dotting

The landscape

Point Reyes resolute

Tamalpais towering

Sometimes

Turbulence sets in

Winds

Whip from the ocean

Carrying fog, moisture

Wild in the night

Mystical in morning

As the trees drip
Like rain

I drive daily
Back to our home site
I look at the torn earth
Where our home stood
First glimpse of soil
After a quarter century
Buried by foundations
Redeemed by fire
The past unraveling
Remembering
The books and art
Hudson River Valley
Dutch Masters
Thomas Cole
Asher Durand
Shishkin's Bears
The great landscapes
Lost in the ash
While life on The Ridge
Remains solid, pastoral
Though we're still
Up in the air
Insurance adjusters
Hanging us out to dry
Giving us time
To rethink our lives
In the aftermath
And I think of Castaway

Tom Hanks, standing
On that crossroad
In the Northern Plains
His life unraveled
Looking North
South, East and West
Horizons, endless
Uprooted
Free to go
Any direction
Contemplating
The next step

Apollo's Fire

We are moving past

The tormented times

Rituals playing out

A sense of renewal

Slowly underway

The mourning is over

We see it in small steps

Waking with the sunrise

Visiting with friends

A growing inner peace

About all that transpired

Going to new places

Revisiting old places

Ventured out today

Went to Weill Hall

Apollo's Fire live

Baroque orchestra

With a chorus line

L'Orfeo Libretto

Monteverdi's masterpiece

Of troubled times

Thought it would be

Forgotten music

On the reinvent

Just a creative distraction

But it touched deep

Into the fire event

Messages laid bare

For the universal ear

About celebrating love
Sorrow
The loss of it all
And the dark road
To recovery
"Abandon all hope, ye who enter."

Monteverdi's Orfeo calls out
From ancient times
As he ventures into the underworld
"Ah bitter fate, ah wicked and cruel destiny
Ah hurtful stars, ah avaricious Heaven
Let no mortal man trust
Fleeting and frail happiness
That soon vanishes and often
After a great ascent a precipice is near."

Orfeo reaches my inner world
Reflections along the way
I can see glimpses of my heart
And of the pathway
Beyond the fires

"Where are you going, my life?
Lo, I follow you—But, who stops me
Alas: do I dream or rave?
What hidden power
Draws me from these beloved horrors
Against my will, and conducts me
To the hateful light?

In Act five
Apollo descends
To lead Orfeo
From stricken demise
To a higher sense

Apollo –
"Too much, too much did you rejoice
in your happy fortune,
now too much you weep
at your bitter, hard lot.
Still do you not know
how nothing that delights down here will last?
In the sun and in the stars …
Let us rise, singing, to heaven,
where true virtue
has due reward, delight and peace."

Walking out of Weill Hall
We both felt a step closer
To that fleeting sense of place
Looking for our Phoenix
In the aftermath
Of Apollo's Fire

Wanderings

Zombies By The Bay

It wasn't supposed to be this way

It's all getting blurry again

Zombies sit on a rented couch

At a rented house

They left The Ridge

The home was sold

Now they're watching waves

On a beautiful bay

Drinking lots of wine

"Looks like it's going to rain"

Says one zombie absently

"Yes it does"

Says the other zombie emptily

No rain in 165 days

Zombies missed that rain

They don't like hot weather

Anymore

It makes them nervous

They loaded up Zombie Dog

In September

After they moved

From The Ridge

To The Bay

Drove the station wagon north

To Portland

They had an ice chest

With food in the car

Zombie Dog in the backseat

His head out the window

At times

Ears flapping

Sniffing the wind

He loved that

Zombies loved to watch him

Love that

I-5 was closed

Delta Fire swept the interstate

Burned cars and trucks

People ran from flames

Zombies read the news

Nonchalantly

All their stuff already burned

Their neighborhood burned

Their city burned

They'd just take another road

There are lots of roads

Lots of fires

Zombies drove up the coast

Then back into the smoke

In Rogue River Valley

"Hah, this is just like a year ago,"

Driver Zombie says

Feeling stuck in Smokeville

Passenger Zombie isn't listening

Or laughing

Just skimming

Portland home prices

On the Internet

Zombie Dog's nose

Cool against the air vent

He didn't feel good
All that smoke again

Rained the whole week
In Portland
Zombies thought it beautiful
And strange
Green and lush
Zombie Dog enjoyed the trip
He curled up on a rented bed
He had his own backyard
And a bowl of food
In Portland
For a week
He was the Zombies'
Best friend
They spent all their time
Together
Since the fires

Now, Zombies are back
At the beautiful bay
Sitting on a rented couch
At a rented house
Staring at the water and clouds
Everything getting blurry again
A stake driven
Into their hearts
At sunrise
When Zombie Dog
Couldn't wake up

He just lay there
Then he was gone

"Looks like it's going to rain"
Says one Zombie absently
"Yes it does"
Says the other Zombie emptily
The fog was rolling in
On that beautiful bay
Clouds were gathering
High overhead
The rains were coming

Wanderings

We went to Point Reyes

The day Jasper died

At sunrise

One year

After the firestorm

We just walked and walked

Toward Tomales Point

No point, really

Just walking

Under that October sky

Like we did in 2017

Right after the fires

Waves washing in

Bull elk bugles

Echoing across

The landscape

No more

Sense of place

Than that night

When we ran

From the flames

Nothing to be said

As we wandered

With the elk

Across the headlands

Looking out

Over the Pacific

Tomales Bay

Marin Hills

In the distance

Imagining a place

Sonoma

Sebastopol

Humboldt

Portland

The Coast

Italy

New Zealand

Uruguay

No place certain

We were just walking

As time passed us by

Settlement Day

One year and a month

After the firestorm

Driving Highway 101

Near Santa Rosa

Noontime

Smoke everywhere

Daylight dimmed down

Brown-copper glow

Residue from Butte County

The Camp Fire

Another firestorm

Another major disaster

Unfolding

100 miles to the northeast

Drifting

Over the mountains

Smothering

The region

The vineyards

Clouds of smoke

Effluents

Bringing back

Those memories

From 2017

Like they are yesterday

Can't shake the chills

Of entrapment

Snared in a recurring

Nightmare

Planned to be
In Chico
This of all weekends
Surprise celebration
To commemorate
A milestone
Of a longtime friend
Everyone's coming
From around the state
Now canceled
As upheaval roars again
Butte Canyon in flames
Paradise is gone
The sky is black
Hard to breathe
Our friend says
They have refugees
From the Camp Fire
Already in their home
Most destructive wildfire
In California history
Again

Stop at Bottle Barn
To restock
Wine's running low
Some customers
Wear air filter masks
Schools closed
Emergency alerts

Buzzing the phone

It's not local smoke!

Reddish sun at noon

You can't see

More than a mile

Phone rings

Screen lights up

Insurance adjuster

From the east

2500 miles away

On car speakers

Hi Mr. G

How are you doing?

Fine, I lied

Not going to mention

Another fire

Seems like

Everyday life

These days

Let's bring this to an end

He says

We're going to pay it out

Close the books

On all this

So you can move on

With your life

My wife and I

Share a glance

Pulling onto 101

A glimpse of light

Through the haze

End of the tunnel
Settlement Day
We keep driving
North

Acknowledgments

First, to those who truly felt a deeper blow from the firestorm and lost loved ones, faced terror, ran in the midst of the fire, were first responders who rushed back into the storm to save families, pets and homes. We'll always be grateful for the heroic efforts by so many and fortunate for the fact that we lived through it.

Greatest thanks to my wife, Oxana, who proved love is stronger than hell. She dug in. She'll never read this book because she lost everything, lived it all and doesn't want to relive it, ever again. She added greatly to the depth of content and concept.

So grateful for Martina and family who stepped up and opened their home to give Chara (Chariste) a loving place and for all Tina's efforts in making that happen. And to Jasper, who carried our spirits all along the way, as far as he could.

Immense gratitude to a circle of long-time friends, editors, writers and fellow readers whom I've shared almost 400 years of accumulative friendships and who encouraged me in this work after reading the manuscript – Katie Sanborn, friend, editor and fellow cyclist on northwest roads for decades; Renee Davis, who designed the book, created all my public presentations over the years and is helping restore my historic book templates, lost in the fire; Robby Jarvis and Randy Bakke, who go back with me to my roots and have always been there for me, and that says it all; Craig Gordon, true buddy in life, business and intellectual pursuit; Connie and Rodney Osborn, who sheltered us after the storm and way before that; Jerilee Olmstead, for her keen editorial sense, fascination with the natural world and shared Humboldt background; Sara Stahl, avid reader and editor from Montana, always in it for the long run; Paula Gobbi, journalist and writer, from London, Rio, Buenos Aires, San Francisco and all places of the world; Joyce Hough and Fred Neighbor, artists in residence of Humboldt County.

Big thanks to Chris McCrum who opened his home on The Ridge to us after the fires which proved a sanctuary of place for recovery and inspiration. And to Joann Steck-Bayat, Staci McGuire and Will Kent who all helped us find the human pathway leading us to Chris and The Ridge. Plus, Chris Kosakowski, who originally built our amazing home

28 years ago, and supported us after the burn-down, as a friend, providing connections and documentation to the past and present; and to his personal efforts that night during the firestorm as a surgeon in the hospital's emergency ward.

To the unforgettable neighbors who lived on our road and who welcomed us in 2014 as the newcomers – and to the fact that we all made it out safely that night along with the nine dogs; Donna and Rod, Allyson and Michael, Diana and Family, RJ and Crystal, Bob and Anita, Victor and Karen and family, Raquel and Jorge and family, Odessa, Levi, Alan and Andrea and family.

And to our circle of longtime friends who offered us homes and support and were always checking in to see how we were doing; we appreciated the many phone calls, the letters, the fly-ins and the visits to our home on The Ridge, an adventure along a series of long, winding and narrow country roads. And the Angel of Wyoming who sparked the holiday ornament array at the darkest hour. To all those who brought food, gifts, humor, wine, books, music, artifacts and photographs from shared times of the past, their own fire stories, life perspectives, bicycles as well as core-help, re-establishing a virtual private network at a remote home base. We never felt isolated.

Recognition to the entire staff of the Press Democrat who devoted heart and soul to the coverage and the aftermath of the North Bay Fires and was justly awarded the Pulitzer Prize for those efforts! Those countless, in-depth articles were incredibly grounding and an invaluable link for myself and I believe the community over the course of the year. We never felt left behind.

The folks at OTR Global, my company from abroad, who rallied in the virtual world, and supported us at every step of the hour, from the fires to recovery; scores of people from all over the country and the globe contacting us, reaching out, visiting us, it meant the world.

And to the online consortium of public and neighborhood Sonoma County networks that proved so valuable and insightful after the fires, insurance webs that illuminated the immense challenge and frustration we all faced in the aftermath, the town hall meetings, the community outreach programs and just the general attitude of the region in providing a supportive atmosphere in the wake of tragedy.

Most incredible, all the folks we met along the way; stories, emotions and experiences shared, sometimes at a retail counter, a chance meeting on the street, a contractor, a vineyard worker, a nurse, doctor, real estate people, service technicians, wine makers, in cafés, gas stations, neighborhood meetings, reunions – there were thousands of stories to be told. This is one of them.

Index of Photographs

All photographs by JHGates

Cover   Bird in a dead tree

9   Our driveway

13   Winter oak corridor along Santa Rosa Creek

23   Palm silhouette in our backyard, just before the fire

93   Burned manzanita and bay trees on hillside

94   Front porch

95   Garden stairs

96   Remnants of our home

97   Scorched manzanita grove; John Deere skeleton

98   Burned bench in what was a grove of green trees; utility trailer for tractor

99   Older manzanita tree base

100 Owl dish from Finland; burned equipment component

101 Collapse of stucco and tiles

102 Voodoo shadows of solar inverter panels, gone

103 Chara (Charista) at home two weeks before the fire

104 Guadalupe palms survived

105 Jasper in the backset at Sea Ranch

106 Wheel barrow; my grandmother's early-1900s Limoges surfaced in the ash

107 Water valves from the well; Alan Tillman's excavators, cleaning debris and digging up the foundations

108 Stucco collapsed on steel and enamel bathtub; the white dripping is melted enamel (1500 degrees)

109	The Ridge: Angel clouds above fog; Jasper walking in the wild grass
110	Storm moving in from the Pacific on The Ridge
111	Author on The Ridge – photo by Oxana
113	An old burned manzanita tree, left over from the 1964 Hanley Fire
165	California poppies, wildflowers and grass emerge in spring, where the house stood
175	Elk grazing at Point Reyes National Seashore – October 2017 after the fires

Other Works by the Author

Falk's Claim
The Life and Death of a Redwood Lumber Town
Moonstone Publishing

Night Crossings
A half-century of maritime encounters with rogue waves in the night while crossing California's notorious Humboldt Bar
Moonstone Publishing

Soviet Passage
Travel Stories and photography from a solo journey across Russia and Siberia in 1984
Summer Run Publishing

Lost Nations (CD)
The Timezone Band
Russian-American worldbeat music collaboration in 1991
Moonstone Publishing

Lost Nations (MP3)
The Timezone Band
Reconstruction and mix translation by Bill Laswell
M.O.D Technologies, New York, NY

www.ingramcontent.com/pod-product-compliance
Lightning Source LLC
Chambersburg PA
CBHW021436080526
44588CB00009B/553